The Author

Derek Walters is one of the few practising specialists of
Chinese Astrology **in the Western hemisphere.**

**Born in the Year of the Fire-Rat, during the Wood-season,
in a Dragon-month, he takes his opportunism from the
Rat, the Wood accounts for his creative side, and the Fire,
a scientific leaning; while the influence of the Dragon is
the stimulus for his interest in astrology.**

Text Copyright © Derek Walters 1988

Compilation Copyright © Pagoda Books 1988

Illustrations: Endpapers, from a Chinese horoscope calendar for
the year 877, courtesy The British Library; p.17, from a Ming Encyclopedia,
dated 1610; page 29, the character for happiness; and page 33, the three
symbols for happiness, dignities and longevity from Researches into
Chinese Superstitions by H. Doré, Shanghai, 1917.

ISBN 0946326 68 1

Printed in Great Britain by
Purnell Book Production Limited

Cast Your Chinese Horoscope

T H E

DOG

犬

D E R E K   W A L T E R S

Contents

Introduction   3

The *DOG* personality   17

How The *DOG* fares in each animal year   21

DOG relationships   25

Your hour of birth   29

Casting a daily horoscope   33

Tables   45

Introduction

*O*ur Destiny! Are we the rulers of our Fate? Are our lives shaped merely by chance circumstances? Or is the future already mapped out for us?

Few people, whatever their beliefs, could honestly say that future events hold little interest for them. Millions of readers worldwide turn to the astrological columns in their newspapers ever day; while at fairs and festivals, fortune-tellers are always sure to be a popular attraction. For the Chinese, meanwhile, a consultation with the seer at the local temple is traditionally regarded a serious matter, not to be undertaken lightly. Indeed, on any day of the week – morning, afternoon and night – Chinese temples, such as the Wong Tai Sin in Kowloon or the ancient Lung Shan in Taipei, are filled with throngs of devout worshippers, who have come to enquire from the monks what the prospects are for future happiness, security, and health.

In ancient times, astrology was a highly secret art, for it was thought that the movements of the stars were messages from the gods to the Emperor, and thus far too important for the eyes and ears of common folk. Every person at the court was represented by one of the stars in the Heavens: and the Emperor's, of course, was the Pole Star, round which, as Confucius said, 'all the other stars make obeisance.' The stars closest to the Pole Star represented the Emperor's family, while round them rotated the stars of the ministers, generals, and nobility. As they twinkled, glimmered or faded, so the fortunes of the court officials were revealed.

With the growth of the Chinese empire, its traders and merchants grew more prosperous; and although they were not important enough to have their own stars in the sky, they were sufficiently well-off to persuade the temple monks to cast their horoscopes for them. It was a crime punishable by death for anyone other than the official court astrologers to study the heavens, but the monks were clever enough to realise that the motions of the stars and planets were sufficiently regular and ordered to enable them to calculate horoscopes based solely on the day of birth. Accordingly, a new branch of astrology developed in China — *Ming Shu*, meaning literally 'the reckoning of Fate'.

In the course of time, the temple astrologer began to play a role as important as a registrar of births, marriages and deaths, and these were the occasions when he was most likely to be in demand: and today, too, Chinese temples have their forecourts and side booths where the temple astrologers can be consulted. Even in mainland China, where 'superstitious practices' are frowned upon by the authorities, orange-robed priests sit patiently in the quiet temples, deftly applying brush-stroke calligraphy to the red paper horoscopes which are still eagerly sought after by the faithful few. In Taiwan, too, old traditions are carefully maintained as a way of life. There, at the great temples, so many astrologers are busy working that their booths overflow the temple grounds into the streets and the subway below, where many of them even have their own private telephones!

According to Chinese tradition, when a child is born, an astrologer is called on to cast horoscopes, and this is usually sealed and kept in a special box throughout the child's life. Often, too, marriages will not be contracted between two families until both parties have consulted their astrologers to ensure that the couple's horoscopes show that they are a compatible pair.

On New Year's Day, Chinese families from Hong Kong to San Francisco, whether or not they are able to go to the expense of employing a professional astrologer to see what the coming year holds in store for them, will certainly buy the new yearly almanac. This is hung at home in a prominent place, where it can be consulted for daily directions and advice on almost every conceivable action, from digging trenches to washing hair. (This might seem odd to the western reader at first; but in fact the western world also has many similar customs with traditional days for doing the laundry, going to market – and even for eating fish or turkey!) The Chinese pay great attention to the almanac's instructions, not just for social convenience, but because it is believed that the penalties for ignoring such daily directions include dire punishment in the world-to-come.

The twelve animals of Chinese astrology

The ancient Chinese first began to study astrology many thousands of years ago, centuries or more before they had made contact with the West: so that by the time that a thriving trade had opened up across the vast continent of Asia, their system of astrology was already firmly established, with quite a different form from the western practice. Even the patterns of stars which shape the constellations were seen quite differently by the ancient Chinese: and the names given to the constellations are significantly different, too. Whereas in the West, many of the names of the stars and constellations have a nautical touch about them, suggesting that the stars were given their names by a people who lived near the sea or who were sea-faring, many Chinese star names, on the other hand, refer to horses and carriages, suggesting a nation that was more at home inland than on the water.

But the most noticeable difference lies at the very heart of popular astrology. In the West, when someone asks about your star-sign, he is really asking which *month* you were born in. The Chinese, however, like to know what *year* you were born in. The twelve animals of Chinese astrology – the so-called 'Chinese Zodiac' – are used to name the different years in one Great Year of twelve ordinary years. So, according to your particular year of birth, you may be a Rat, Ox, Tiger or Hare; a Dragon, Snake, Horse or Sheep; a Monkey, Rooster, Dog or Pig.

How, when, or why these animals were chosen to represent their particular years is a mystery which perplexes scholars to this day. Legend says that the Buddha summoned all the animals, and that these twelve were the only ones which answered. It is more likely, however, that these animal names were carefully chosen by ancient astrologers because they seemed to be the best ones to represent the characteristics of people born in those years, and also indicated what the events of coming years might be like.

As you become acquainted with the characteristics of each animal year, remember that the Chinese interpretation is often very different from western ideas. Some people find it far from flattering to learn that they were born in Rat or Pig years, for example: but to the Chinese, the Rat is the symbol of ingenuity; and the Pig, a sign of comfort. You can discover more about your own animal type on pages 17-20; while if you turn to the section beginning on page 21, you will find how you are likely to fare in each different animal year.

Yin and Yang signs

The twelve animal signs are conveniently grouped into six pairs – the first of each pair considered to have *yang* or active attributes, the second possessing softer *yin* qualities. Thus, the creative Rat is paired with the practical Ox; the competitive Tiger with the diplomatic Hare; the exuberant Dragon with the prudent Snake; the convivial Horse with the rather astute Rooster; and the faithful Dog with the caring Pig.

According to Chinese beliefs, all things are made from differing proportions of *yin* and *yang*. It is even sometimes said that these two forces correspond to 'female' and 'male'; but in reality, they are only terms of convenience. Thus in any one personality, *yin* and *yang* represent the opposing sides of human character, the passive and the active, the imaginative and the logical, as well as the creative and the destructive.

Personality revealed

Each pair of animal signs further combines to form one of the six aspects of destiny known to astrologers as 'Houses.' Not only do these help to paint a character portrait, they also reveal the likely trends of fortune for different periods of time – years, months, days, or hours – which are associated with each animal.

The Rat and Ox represent beginnings and completions of projects in the *House of Construction*; the Tiger and the Hare symbolise the aggressive and diplomatic paths to personal achievement in the *House of Expansion*; the Dragon and the Snake reflect the extrovert and introspective sides of personality in the *House of Mystery*; the Horse and Sheep reveal the basic differences in interests shown by both sexes in the *House of Gender*; craftsmanship and flair are the two qualities essential to success represented by the Monkey and the Rooster in the *House of Career*; and finally, the Dog, symbolising friendship and protection, and the Pig symbolising the home, its comforts, and also offspring, belong to the *House of Family*.

Many people, when they first encounter Chinese astrology, find it hard to accept the general principle that everyone born in a particular year will have the same basic characteristics. But in fact this is one of Chinese astrology's most convincing factors: and teachers, in particular, are very apt to observe that each school year's intake seems to have its own inherent characteristics.

There are also a number of ways by which the general characteristics of each animal-type can be refined to give a detailed character assessment of each individual. For just as anyone familiar with western astrology will know that the hour of birth reveals the 'ascendant' of the horoscope, the Chinese consider that the time at which person was born has an important bearing on future career and happiness. Other aspects which help to paint a more accurate picture of personality and fate are given by the month or season of birth: and the animal-types associated with each month may either strengthen or weaken the characteristics of the year-type. Thus, someone born in a Rat year would have his Rat characteristics emphasized if born in a Rat month, but toned down if born in the Horse month – the Rat's opposite sign. The Chinese calendar is regulated by the phases of the Moon, and is therefore extremely complicated; but you will be able to get a good idea of which animal is associated with your particular birth month from the table on page 12.

Compatibility between animal types

Once you are familiar with your own animal sign, you will no doubt want to know the signs of others close to you, and then to establish the nature and extent of your compatibility.

There is a simple way to do this. If the names of the twelve animals are placed in order (Rat, Ox, Tiger, Hare, Dragon, Snake, Horse, Sheep, Monkey, Rooster, Dog, Pig) at the twelve positions of the hours of a clock-face, with your own birth-year animal at the twelve o'clock position, then the most compatible signs will be at the four o'clock and eight o'clock positions, compatible signs at two and ten o'clock, poor compatibility at three and nine o'clock, and adversity shown at the six o'clock position.

The Twelve Chinese Months and their Associated Animals

First month   approximating to February: *the Tiger*

Second month   approximating to March: *the Hare*
    (The Hare month includes the Spring Equinox)

Third month   approximating to April: *the Dragon*

Fourth month   approximating to May: *the Snake*

Fifth month   approximating to June: *the Horse*
    (The Horse month includes the Summer Solstice)

Sixth month   approximating to July: *the Sheep*

Seventh month   approximating to August: *the Monkey*

Eighth month   approximating to September: *the Rooster*
    (The Rooster month includes the Autumn Equinox)

Ninth month   approximating to October: *the Dog*

Tenth month   approximating to November: *the Pig*

Eleventh month approximating to December: *the Rat*
    (The Rat month includes the Winter Solstice)

Twelfth month   approximating to January: *the Ox*

Broadly-speaking, the most compatible signs fall into four groups of three: the Rat, Dragon, and Monkey; the Ox, Snake, and Rooster; the Tiger, Dog and Horse; and the Pig, Hare and Sheep. More detailed remarks on your relationships with other people, whether in business, within the family, in friendship or in romance, can be found on pages 25-28.

But to make a more specific comparison of two personalities, it is also important to take into account the interaction of the Five Elements.

The Five Elements

The Chinese sages of old taught that the Universe is kept in order by Five Elements – Wood, Fire, Earth, Metal and Water – and that one gives rise to the next in regular succession, or as the Chinese say: 'Wood burns, producing Fire; Fire leaves ash – or Earth – from which Metal is mined; Metal melts, like Water; and Water feeds growing Wood'; after which the whole cycle begins again.

Similarly, the order of the Five Elements can be likened to the progress of the year as it passes through five 'seasons', each associated with one of the elements. Spring, season of growth and creation, belongs to Wood; the hot season is governed by

Fire; the middle of the year, by the Earth element; the harvest, when ploughs cut into the Earth, by Metal; and finally, the cold, wet season, by Water.

In the Chinese calendar, years are counted in pairs according to the elements. Thus 1984 and 1985 were ruled by the Wood element, 1986 and 1987 by the Fire element, and so on. In this way, each year has both an animal name and an element; so that someone born in a particular year can be described not only as a particular animal type but also by the relevant element. This makes it possible to outline character assessments in greater detail: and just how the five elements influence your own particular animal sign is explained more fully on pages 19-20.

Compatibility between the element types

The usual order of the Five Elements is the 'generative' order, in which each element 'generates' the next in the series: and as a general rule, it can be said that two people will be compatible if their influencing elements stand in the generative order – a Wood-type and a Water-type, for instance. But there is also a 'destructive' order (Wood – Earth – Water – Fire – Metal), in which each successive element overpowers the other, and such combinations are usually found to be less fortunate. (Wood is said to absorb the goodness from Earth; Earth sullies Water; Water quenches Fire; Fire melts Metal; and Metal chops down Wood.)

From these two orders, it is easy to imagine how one element type may either help or hinder another. Positively, a Wood-type may provide the Fire person with resources; the Fire-type may stimulate the obstinate Earth; Earth may give stability to the rash Metal-type; Metal may give active support to the dreaming Water personality; and Water may provide the knowledge from which the Wood-type is able to create.

Conversely, the Wood-type may will be a drain on the Earth's reserves, perhaps of patience or even materially; an Earth-type could cause damage to Water's reputation; Water may quench the Fire-type's enthusiasm; Fire would be a very formidable opponent for the normally assertive Metal-type, who in turn might harrass Wood.

But what of the future, whatever your animal-type? Chinese astrologers maintain that the success or failure of plans can be foreseen by charting the progress of the Five Elements – whether they are dominant, recessive, waxing or waning: and by comparing the pattern of the Elements of a particular day with those of your own birth-date, Chinese astrologers are able to advise whether the day is likely to prove favourable or otherwise.

Now, with the help of this guide, you will be able to chart your own daily horoscope aspect from the step-by-step instructions given on pages 33–37.

Some people may claim that they do not wish to know what the future holds in store for them. But if there is danger ahead, is it not better to be forewarned? And if there is happiness, will it not give encouragement? Often we are faced with crises and decisions. By perusing your daily horoscope aspect, and taking into consideration the prevailing fortunate elements, problems and dilemmas can often be untangled, and the right direction made clearer.

It is my sincere hope that the knowledge and advice gathered for you from the many friends I have met during my travels to the temples and monasteries throughout China and the Far East will bring you a deeper insight and understanding of your true self, and your relationship with the world about you.

Derek Walters

戌神將名展子江

The *DOG*
Personality

*F*idelity, honesty, and humour are high priorities for the typical Dog character. Such a likeable personality easily makes friends, forging long-lasting relationships: and being a steady worker, the Dog becomes a trusted and valued employee.

But conservatism can be a handicap. The Dog tolerates considerable hardship and inconvenience rather than making major changes: and when circumstances force the issue, it takes a long time to adjust, no matter how improved conditions may be. For the Dog, nothing is ever as good as it was 'in the old days.'

Intensely defensive where friends and family are concerned, the Dog will not stand by while others are maligned. Otherwise, the Dog is a sympathetic listener to other people's woes, always ready with a shoulder to cry on.

Rare displays of violent anger are almost always justified, but wrongs are quickly forgotten and resentment only borne against those outside the intimate circle of family and friends.

Born in the Year of the Dog

Chris Bonnington, Charles Bronson, Winston Churchill,
Judy Garland, Golda Meir, Mother Teresa

How the Five Elements affect
the DOG Personality

The WOOD-Dog
14 Feb 1934-3 Feb 1935,   10 Feb 1994-30 Jan 1995

Rustic, practical, and active, the Dog born in a Wood year will feel happiest when pottering outside the home, and would make an excellent gardener, if only the time allowed. The Wood-Dog prefers casual dress, enjoying outdoor pursuits; and in love, is romantic and chivalrous. With a partner born in a Water year, marriage should prove to be prosperous.

The FIRE-Dog
2 Feb 1946-21 Jan 1947

The element Fire enhances the liveliness of the typical Dog. Quick-witted and intelligent, as well as being physically active, such a character will enjoy working on the mechanical trappings of the house. With a restless nature, and sometimes aggressive, the Fire-Dog will be fiercely protective towards the home. In love, this personality is demanding, and not always entirely faithful, but will settle down very happily with someone born in an Earth year.

The EARTH-Dog
18 Feb 1958-7 Feb 1959

The Earth-Dog may be drawn to property development as a career, as all the aptitude for house construction is contained in this astrological sign. This personality is authoritative at home, stressing the importance of integrity. The Earth-Dog is unromantic, though nevertheless tender. The ideal marriage partner would also be born in an Earth year.

The METAL-Dog
10 Feb 1910-29 Jan 1911,   6 Feb 1970-26 Jan 1971

The defensive characteristics of the Dog personality are intensified by the Metal element, symbol of the military; and many Metal-Dog types are drawn to the uniformed services or professions. Love may not be the first necessity of life, but loyalty is. The ideal companion in life would be born in an Earth year, as such a person would have the steadfastness that the Metal-Dog demands.

The WATER-Dog
28 Jan 1922-15 Feb 1923,   25 Jan 1982-12 Feb 1983

The Water element heightens the Dog-personality's natural faithfulness. Such people would be happiest working from home, where they would feel secure. They are fond of expressing their affections, and are hurt if their partners do not do the same. Their ideal life-companion would be born in a Metal or Wood Year.

How the *DOG*
fares in each animal year

In the Year of the *RAT*, *19 Feb 1996–6 Feb 1997*

This is a good year for those born in the Year of the Dog; not one of the best, but better than usual. The Rat Year, being the start of the twelve-year cycle, brings about growth and expansion, and the Dog will benefit by investigating possibilities this positive period offers.

In the Year of the *OX*, *7 Feb 1997–27 Jan 1998*

This is not the best of years for the Dog-native, for the Ox stands in the way of the Dog's ambitions, leading to resentment and ill-feeling. It is advisable to curtail expense and to let ambitious schemes lie fallow. There will be improvements in the following year, however, with benefits accruing in the year after that.

In the Year of the *TIGER*, *28 Jan 1998–15 Feb 1999*

Good fortune attends the Dog all the way this year, and it is a happy time all round. Promotion is indicated, and business interests expand successfully. Dog personalities will have a more than usually active social life, and there are highlights in the romantic field. It is a good year for travel.

In the Year of the *HARE*, *16 Feb 1999–4 Feb 2000*

Much of the impetus of last year carries over, and many projects begun then are brought to fulfilment. For those just setting out in marriage, the arrival of a new family member means considering the need to move house, and it would be wisest to do this during the current year.

In the Year of the *DRAGON*, *17 Feb 1988–5 Feb 1989*

Dog-personalities have to fend for themselves just now, as they contend with a seemingly endless number of obstacles. In matters of the heart, there may be a few tears; in finances, a few worries. But happily, this difficult phase is a passing one.

In the Year of the *SNAKE*, *6 Feb 1989–26 Jan 1990*

This is a moderate year, with the promise of financial security, but with a few worries still standing in the way. Fortunately, the position is becoming increasingly stable. This would be an ideal period to start planning ahead, or to save for some ambitious project which can be put into effect next year.

In the Year of the *HORSE*, *27 Jan 1990–14 Feb 1991*

The Dog and the Horse are stable companions; so it is only to be expected that The Year of the Horse should be an especially good year for those born in the Year of the Dog. There is a very strong indication of travel either for a well-deserved vacation, or for business reasons.

In the Year of the *SHEEP*, *15 Feb 1991–3 Feb 1992*

Those born in the Year of the Dog enter a period of conflict when the Year Marker, the *T'ai Sui*, enters the Sheep sector. The home, which the Dog symbolically guards, is in danger, as is the area in which it stands. Expensive renovation seems to threaten. With the House of Expansion being the only sector favourably aspected, the answer may lie in moving altogether. Despite this, family life shows up well.

In the Year of the *MONKEY*, *4 Feb 1992–22 Jan 1993*

This is a moderately good period for those born in the Year of the Dog, and the gains at the end of this year will be quite considerable. Improvements are made to the home, and social life is very busy. But business takes up a lot of time; and, while ample recompense is made financially, personal life may suffer in some way.

In the Year of the *ROOSTER*, *23 Jan 1993–9 Feb 1994*

The Year of the Rooster is an extraordinarily eventful one for the Dog-type. There are some remarkably good strokes of fortune, interspersed with periods of personal conflict. Plans for improvements to the house, or relocation, for instance, cause clashes of opinion.

In the Year of the *DOG*, *10 Feb 1994–30 Jan 1995*

As protector of the home, the Dog may decide to move house or perhaps carry out significant improvements to present accommodation this year. In either case, the moment will be right, even if it is not possible to complete plans for another year. Social life and commercial opportunities are at their best.

In the Year of the *PIG*, *31 Jan 1995–18 Feb 1996*

The Dog will find this a happy year, with considerable activity at home. Matters do not always run entirely smoothly, however, and special attention may need to be given to children. There will be anxieties over travel. With commercial dealings moving rather slowly now, a stroke of good fortune will prove doubly welcome.

DOG *Relationships*

Find out how you relate to each
of the twelve animal signs, with specific reference
to interaction within the family, in business
and in romance. The tables on pages 46-48
provide a guide to each animal year.

with the Rat   In personal matters and in business dealings, there are likely to be some conflicts, but this relationship is more than able to weather any storms. The Rat-child will bring his or her Dog-parent great joy.

with the Ox   There are likely to be some difficulties here, with each partner finding the other obstructive. A degree of mutual indulgence would benefit all business and personal relationships. Be warned; the Ox-child may get sullen and obstinate if the Dog-parent tries to interfere too much.

with the Tiger   This is an ideal partnership for a fun-loving couple, with many shared interests. In business, a good working arrangement also exists. The Dog-parent will be very proud of the Tiger-child.

with the Hare   If this loving relationship is based mainly on physical attraction, what of it? Business partnerships, however, need a much firmer foundation. The Hare-child may find it difficult to communicate with the Dog-parent on important matters.

with the Dragon This is an awkward relationship since the Dog does not regard the Dragon's flamboyance sympathetically. In business, too, there is some mistrust. The Dog-parent may not fully appreciate the Dragon-child's ability, either.

with the Snake This is not the best of relationships, there being few affinities to indicate a lasting partnership. Business ventures are rarely certain, either. The parental Dog should also guard against misunderstanding the Snake-child's ambitions.

with the Horse This is by far the most ideal partnership for the Dog, with mutual understanding and shared pleasures. In business, this is also a strong team. The Horse-child will amply reward the parental Dog's kindness in time, too.

with the Sheep In romance, there will be tears; in business, conflict: and yet there is much for others to envy in this love-hate relationship. The Sheep-child may feel lost at home unless the parent-Dog is ever attentive.

with the Monkey This waggish duo enjoy life to the full. Romantically, they make an engaging couple; and in business, their unconventional approach usually succeeds. The Monkey-child will be very active, and may seem excessively so to the Dog-parent. A love of mischief is the key-note in this relationship.

with the Rooster Proverbially this is a poor relationship, and indeed affection has to be very strong to bind these two together. In romance, there are misunderstandings; in business, mistrust. The Rooster-child is very independent, the Dog-parent will find.

with another Dog In love and business, Dog partners know each other inside out. The Dog-child will also be the closest to the Dog-parent in any family.

with the Pig This should be a safe, long-lasting, but unexciting relationship both in romance and business. The Pig-child is affectionate, and will be well-loved by the parental Dog.

How the Hour of Birth affects the Fate of the *DOG* Personality

Born during the *RAT* hour (11pm-1am)

Generally adaptable and practical, you may well often look on your career as a means of establishing greater comfort at home, which may be regularly improved or upgraded. Though you are sometimes restless, domestic life will be very happy.

Born during the *OX* hour (1am-3am)

After a period of insecurity, considerable effort will be put into establishing a secure home. In romantic life, early disillusionment will be followed by a happy partnership. Good fortune and fame arrive through an unexpected incident.

Born during the *TIGER* hour (3am-5am)

The position regarding foreign travel is very favourable: and as you are adventurous, you may well seek romance or fortune abroad. But domestic bliss is not indicated, though a good marriage is.

Born during the *HARE* hour (5am-7am)

The signs reveal success through moveable assets and interests in medical care; and the ideal career would fuse both these elements. Public recognition comes late in life. Children will be a source of great pride.

Born during the *DRAGON* hour (7am-9am)

Speculation may well bring speedy profits; but there is a chance of losing everything in a false move. Take care with investments, and never be tempted to risk everything. Romantic involvements cause occasional heartaches. Health is sound.

Born during the *SNAKE* hour (9am-11am)

The choice of career may be one in uniform, where quick-thinking and intelligence are vital, suggesting the police, the air force or a technical area, and public recognition is likely. Domestic and family matters cannot always be the first consideration in life, the Dog born during the Snake hour will find.

Born during the *HORSE* hour (11am-1pm)

You are likely to be defensive, very set in your ways and opinions, and highly protective towards the family, or other social group. Marriage is likely to be early, and rewarding.

Born during the *SHEEP* hour (1pm-3pm)

As a home-loving person, you will probably put the family ahead of career prospects or personal advancement. Though wealth and riches may be elusive, happiness is assured.

Born during the *MONKEY* hour (3pm-5pm)

The signs are excellent for those dealing with crafts, and particularly furnishings. A comfortable home and happy romantic life are indicated, but there may be worries concerning the family.

Born during the *ROOSTER* hour (5pm-7pm)

Domestic conflict and disputes within the family may cause obstacles on the road to personal success. Those in pursuit of a public career will no doubt battle ahead, despite set-backs. Wealth, fortune, and fame are all within reach.

Born during the *DOG* hour (7pm-9pm)

The positive aspects of the Dog personality – trust, loyalty, and protectiveness – are all emphasized, revealing someone anxious to care and provide for the family. There is no shortage of love, but it may be necessary to spend time working away from home.

Born during the *PIG* hour (9pm-11pm)

A long and contented life is promised. Romance will blossom, leading to an early marriage and a stable home life. Marriage and career may be combined, resulting in a happy partnership.

Casting a daily horoscope

*T*he Chinese have always been very down-to-earth in their approach to astrology; and while they find it fascinating to learn about their inner selves and to know how they stand in their personal relationships, they are much more likely to expect an astrologer to give them sound, practical advice on everyday matters.

Chinese astrology is certainly able to do much more than reveal the complexities of your personality. Indeed, by drafting an individual daily horoscope forecast, it is possible to discover which days will be best suited for business and social life, when you may need to take special care, when you would do best to stay at home rather than embarking on a long journey, or when you are likely to meet with particularly good fortune.

On the pages that follow, you will find the basic method for casting your own personal daily horoscope, carefully set out, step by step. No mathematical prowess is needed, just an ability to add and subtract a few simple figures. These straightforward calculations will enable you to find the cyclic number for your date of birth, and any other date this century. (These numbers are an exact match with those published in the official Chinese astrological calendar, the oldest in the world, and still in continuous use after more than three thousand years.) These two numbers are then compared to find the *aspect number* which reveals the daily forecast given in the final section.

How to Calculate Your Own Personal Daily Horoscope Aspect

(Note: The Chinese day begins at 11pm: so if you were born between 11pm and midnight, base your calculations on the day following your birthdate.)

Take a piece of paper, preferably lined, and write the letters A to K in a column down the left-hand side.

Finding the cyclic number for your date of birth

[A] At A on your sheet of paper, write the *date* of the month of your birth: i.e. if you were born on 12th April, write 12.

[B] Using Table I on page 45, find the code number for your month of birth and write this at B.

[C] Using Table II on page 45, find the code number for your year of birth and write this at C.

[D] If you were born on or after February 29th during a leap-year, put 1 at D. Otherwise put O. (A leap year is one which is divisible by 4; 1988 is therefore a leap year).

[E] Add the figures at A, B, C and D.
If the result is 121 or more, subtract 120; if the figure is between 61 and 120, subtract 60. Write the result at E.

This is the *cyclic number for your birthdate*.

Finding the cyclic number for any date this century

You will need to follow the same procedure outlined in steps A to D to find the cyclic number for any required day this century.

[F] Write the *date* of the month of the required date at F.

[G] Write the *monthly* code number for the required month at G.

[H] Write the *yearly* code number for the required year at H.

[I] Write the figure 1 at I, if a leap-year adjustment is required. Otherwise put O.

[J] Add the figures at F, G, H and I.

If the total is 121 or more, subtract 120; if the figure is between 61 and 120, subtract 60. Write the result at J.

This is the *cyclic number for the required date*.

Finding your personal daily aspect number

First note whether the cyclic number for your birthdate (E) is *yang* (an *odd* number) or *yin* (an even number.)

(i) If the cyclic number for your birthdate (E) is *yang* (odd):
>from the cyclic number for the required date (J)
>SUBTRACT
>the cyclic number for the birthdate (E).
>(Note. If J is less then E, first add 60.)
>Write your result at K.

(ii) If the cyclic number for your birthdate (E) is *yin* (even):
>from the cyclic number for the birthdate (E)
>SUBTRACT
>the cyclic number for the required date (J).
>(Note. If E is less than J, first add 60.)
>Write your result at K.

The figure at K is your *Personal Daily Aspect Number*. Now turn to pages 38–44 to find your own personal forecast for the required date.

Your Personal Daily Horoscope Aspects

[0] *See aspect 60.*

[1] It will be a wonderful day for the Dog, with many enjoyable activities in store. If there is a cause for celebration, today will be remembered for a long time. Any matters connected with construction or rebuilding in the home are very favourably aspected.

[2] The Dog will find this an ideal day for long journeys. Conditions are less ideal for routine activities, however. Do not try to do too many things at once.

[3] There are highly favourable prospects for your ideas regarding home changes. Some set-backs regarding the signing of documents, however, could arise. Business runs smoothly, but avoid unusual or novel activities today.

[4] You should take advice if you are planning changes to your home. Leave any decisions until you feel more confident. Do not be disheartened by your family's adverse criticisms.

[5] This is an ideal day for most business affairs, especially if they concern travel or legal matters.

[6] While the day passes peaceably enough, you will not get through everything you wanted to do. Do not act too hastily with personal plans today.

[7] The Dog's prospects for today are improved. There could be some set-backs regarding travel plans, however. A chance of promotion and a better financial position may arise.

[8] Despite minor set-backs, you will succeed today. So go about achieving your objectives with confidence.

[9] This is a particularly demanding, but nevertheless highly successful day. Be prepared to put a lot of effort into your activities today. Try to avoid disputes.

[10] During this stimulating day, you will possibly feel restless, and start to make travel plans. Go ahead with confidence.

[11] Use your knowledge of present conditions to put your plans into action. Keep on sure ground, and stick to family matters.

[12] This is a good day for the Dog to sign papers and documents. Finances may seem more secure, but try to keep expenditure to a minimum.

[13] Conditions are favourable for all matters to do with your family, social, and personal life. There could be some set-backs regarding career prospects, however.

[14] Matters today remain fairly stable, and there is an improved position with respect to finances, personal correspondence and the signing of documents.

[15] It is a day of mixed blessings. Try to avoid creating jealousy among friends and colleagues, and act calmly when faced with a trying situation today.

[16] It would be advisable not to get too involved in activities concerning strangers. There will be success in business, but best achievements will come from your own efforts.

[17] This is a highly favourable day for the Dog in all matters concerning travel, business, and commercial transactions. Your successes may cause resentment, however. Leisure plans are highlighted at mid-day.

[18] There is improvement with respect to matters affecting land and all long-term projects which have been going for some time. Avoid unnecessary journeys.

[19] This is a good day for reading, conversation, or artistic work. You should take advice if you are worried about your health.

[20] Push ahead with your personal plans. It will be a smooth-running day; and personal success is in sight, if not actually achieved today. There will be news for you late at night.

[21] While all the signs are for the most part favourable, avoid commercial transactions today. You may encounter a few obstacles regarding a legal position.

[22] A personal ambition is realised today, and there are signs of improvement in your financial situation. But be prepared for a frustrating time, and keep your head. Avoid unnecessary travel.

[23] All practical matters will be successful today, and finances will be sound, you should find.

[24] Act positively today in a difficult personal situation; and disregard personal remarks. Prospects regarding your family are highly favourable.

[25] Some discussion holds up proposals regarding a change of location. Good news arrives in the afternoon.

[26] You may find the morning stimulating, and will work hard as a result. But, in legal matters, there is only moderate satisfaction.

[27] There are highly favourable prospects for family matters today. You will also surmount a major obstacle, although not without a struggle on the way.

[28] Although you will achieve success with respect to your financial prospects; there may be objections to your plans in other directions. Generally, however, it is a good day.

[29] Don't organize anything out-of-the-ordinary today, as some unexpected obstacles may arise. It is important for you that matters remain stable.

[30] You will find this an excellent day for outdoor work. Avoid any expenditure if possible.

[31] This will be an enjoyable day, and leisure activities are highlighted. There are also very favourable prospects for matters relating to friends.

[32] Matters go smoothly at work and at home. You should take advice regarding the signing of documents, however, and be sure to watch finances.

[33] There will be an improved position regarding career prospects. It is also a good day for making small purchases.

[34] In practical matters, conditions are very favourable. Do not be disheartened if results are not forthcoming immediately.

[35] Anything to do with business is highlighted for the Dog today, and progress will be made with respect to career and promotion.

There could also be good news regarding family matters. Avoid gambling today.

[36] There are ideal conditions at home today. You can also expect a visit from a stranger.

[37] Avoid becoming anxious over minor details today, and try not to take matters too seriously.

[38] Be careful in your dealings with strangers and the unfamiliar generally, especially in the morning.

[39] Conditions improve, enabling progress to be made. The day will be successful in most respects, particularly with regards to home improvements.

[40] The Dog will find this to be a good day for dealing with people; but practical activities run into snags. There are particularly encouraging results in any matters involving children.

[41] This is a favourable day for all kinds of activity. Be prepared to find yourself doing more than you had planned. Your expenditure will be greater than expected, too.

[42] Try to take things easily today. Rash actions may lead to accidents, and you may not be able to cope capably with the heavy demands made upon you.

[43] This is a good day for making plans, and for anything involving construction, artistic activities, or travel. It is much better to be busy, and leave socializing, romance and leisure pursuits for another time.

[44] This is a good, steady day when you will have confidence in both business and personal relationships.

[45] Use the favourable circumstances surrounding you to their best advantage. You will be best working away from home today, but do not waste time in unnecessary travelling.

[46] It will be an unfavourable day for dealings with colleagues, family, or circumstances where you have to assert yourself. But by keeping out of the spotlight you will be able to learn from other people's mistakes.

[47] You will find yourself involved in considerable activity today, so be prepared for the extra demands on you. In the end, however, the results will be well worth it.

[48] It will be both a stimulating and inspiring day. Renewed strength and confidence will help you to obtain your objectives. There is a chance of promotion and recognition, too.

[49] Conditions remain generally unchanged, and all the minor irritations are still with you. You will just have to tolerate people's awkwardness a little longer. Stick to the tried and trusted.

[50] This is an ideal day for the Dog's leisure activities, while romance is a possibility. Business ticks over; but don't organize anything too demanding for today.

[51] You could find yourself involved in a lot of strenuous leisure activity today, and the accent appears to be on enjoyment. Be careful not to overspend.

[52] This is a day when things may seem to get on top of you. Try not to get involved in open-ended situations. Plan ahead carefully and keep objectives short-term.

[53] This is a good day for recreation, social activities, dealing with colleagues and friends, and any romantic plans you may have. A financial windfall is also a possibility.

[54] The signs are generally harmonious and peaceful. At the end of the day, you may not have achieved as much as usual, but the rest will have done you no harm.

[55] Conditions are very favourable today in all respects for the Dog; and in particular, home and family matters are highlighted.

[56] Renewed vigour and self-confidence will enable you to succeed in business and personal matters today.

[57] It will be a highly successful day, but you will be glad when it is all over. Try to snatch a few moments to yourself.

[58] Conditions are better today for quiet creative planning, rather than constructive, practical matters. Health is good. Avoid gambling, or anything involving financial risk.

[59] Use the present stable conditions to their best advantage. This is a good time for looking over any contracts involving land, or for anything involving the family's welfare.

[60][0] Proceed with confidence. Prospects for health, travel, home-life, business and romance are all excellent.

TABLE I
Code number for the month

Month	Jan	Feb	Mar	April	May	June	July	Aug	Sept	Oct	Nov	Dec
Code	0	31	59	30	0	31	1	32	3	35	4	34

TABLE II
Code number for the year

Year	1901	1902	1903	1904	1905	1906	1907	1908	1909	1910	1911	1912
Code	15	20	25	30	36	41	46	51	57	2	7	12

Year	1913	1914	1915	1916	1917	1918	1919	1920	1921	1922	1923	1924
Code	18	23	28	33	39	44	49	54	0	5	10	15

Year	1925	1926	1927	1928	1929	1930	1931	1932	1933	1934	1935	1936
Code	21	26	31	36	42	47	52	57	3	8	13	18

Year	1937	1938	1939	1940	1941	1942	1943	1944	1945	1946	1947	1948
Code	24	29	34	39	45	50	55	0	6	11	16	21

Year	1949	1950	1951	1952	1953	1954	1955	1956	1957	1958	1959	1960
Code	27	32	37	42	48	53	58	3	9	14	19	24

Year	1961	1962	1963	1964	1965	1966	1967	1968	1969	1970	1971	1972
Code	30	35	40	45	51	56	1	6	12	17	22	27

Year	1973	1974	1975	1976	1977	1978	1979	1980	1981	1982	1983	1984
Code	33	38	43	48	54	59	4	9	15	20	25	30

Year	1985	1986	1987	1988	1989	1990	1991	1992	1993	1994	1995	1996
Code	36	41	46	51	57	2	7	12	18	23	28	33

Year	1997	1998	1999	2000
Code	39	44	49	54

The Chinese Calendar

19 Feb 1901 – 7 Feb 1902
Metal-Ox

8 Feb 1902 – 28 Jan 1903
Water-Tiger

29 Jan 1903 – 15 Feb 1904
Water-Hare

16 Feb 1904 – 3 Feb 1905
Wood-Dragon

4 Feb 1905 – 24 Jan 1906
Wood-Snake

25 Jan 1906 – 12 Feb 1907
Fire-Horse

13 Feb 1907 – 1 Feb 1908
Fire-Sheep

2 Feb 1908 – 21 Jan 1909
Earth-Monkey

22 Jan 1909 – 9 Feb 1910
Earth-Rooster

10 Feb 1910 – 29 Jan 1911
Metal-Dog

30 Jan 1911 – 17 Feb 1912
Metal-Pig

18 Feb 1912 – 5 Feb 1913
Water-Rat

6 Feb 1913 – 25 Jan 1914
Water-Ox

26 Jan 1914 – 13 Feb 1915
Wood-Tiger

14 Feb 1915 – 2 Feb 1916
Wood-Hare

3 Feb 1916 – 22 Jan 1917
Fire-Dragon

23 Jan 1917 – 10 Feb 1918
Fire-Snake

11 Feb 1918 – 31 Jan 1919
Earth-Horse

1 Feb 1919 – 19 Feb 1920
Earth-Sheep

20 Feb 1920 – 7 Feb 1921
Metal-Monkey

8 Feb 1921 – 27 Jan 1922
Metal-Rooster

28 Jan 1922 – 15 Feb 1923
Water-Dog

16 Feb 1923 – 4 Feb 1924
Water-Pig

5 Feb 1924 – 24 Jan 1925
Wood-Rat

25 Jan 1925 – 12 Feb 1926
Wood-Ox

13 Feb 1926 – 1 Feb 1927
Fire-Tiger

2 Feb 1927 – 22 Jan 1928
Fire-Hare

23 Jan 1928 – 9 Feb 1929
Earth-Dragon

8 Feb 1940 – 26 Jan 1941
Metal-Dragon

27 Jan 1952 – 13 Feb 1953
Water-Dragon

10 Feb 1929 – 29 Jan 1930
Earth-Snake

27 Jan 1941 – 14 Feb 1942
Metal-Snake

14 Feb 1953 – 2 Feb 1954
Water-Snake

30 Jan 1930 – 16 Feb 1931
Metal-Horse

15 Feb 1942 – 4 Feb 1943
Water-Horse

3 Feb 1954 – 23 Jan 1955
Wood-Horse

17 Feb 1931 – 5 Feb 1932
Metal-Sheep

5 Feb 1943 – 24 Jan 1944
Water-Sheep

24 Jan 1955 – 11 Feb 1956
Wood-Sheep

6 Feb 1932 – 25 Jan 1933
Water-Monkey

25 Jan 1944 – 12 Feb 1945
Wood-Monkey

12 Feb 1956 – 30 Jan 1957
Fire-Monkey

26 Jan 1933 – 13 Feb 1934
Water-Rooster

13 Feb 1945 – 1 Feb 1946
Wood-Rooster

31 Jan 1957 – 17 Feb 1958
Fire-Rooster

14 Feb 1934 – 3 Feb 1935
Wood-Dog

2 Feb 1946 – 21 Jan 1947
Fire-Dog

18 Feb 1958 – 7 Feb 1959
Earth-Dog

4 Feb 1935 – 23 Jan 1936
Wood-Pig

22 Jan 1947 – 9 Feb 1948
Fire-Pig

8 Feb 1959 – 27 Jan 1960
Earth-Pig

24 Jan 1936 – 10 Feb 1937
Fire-Rat

10 Feb 1948 – 28 Jan 1949
Earth-Rat

28 Jan 1960 – 14 Feb 1961
Metal-Rat

11 Feb 1937 – 30 Jan 1938
Fire-Ox

29 Jan 1949 – 16 Feb 1950
Earth-Ox

15 Feb 1961 – 4 Feb 1962
Metal-Ox

31 Jan 1938 – 18 Feb 1939
Earth-Tiger

17 Feb 1950 – 5 Feb 1951
Metal-Tiger

5 Feb 1962 – 24 Jan 1963
Water-Tiger

19 Feb 1939 – 7 Feb 1940
Earth-Hare

6 Feb 1951 – 26 Jan 1952
Metal-Hare

25 Jan 1963 – 12 Feb 1964
Water-Hare

13 Feb 1964 – 1 Feb 1965
Wood-Dragon

2 Feb 1965 – 20 Jan 1966
Wood-Snake

21 Jan 1966 – 8 Feb 1967
Fire-Horse

9 Feb 1967 – 29 Jan 1968
Fire-Sheep

30 Jan 1968 – 16 Feb 1969
Earth-Monkey

17 Feb 1969 – 5 Feb 1970
Earth-Rooster

6 Feb 1970 – 26 Jan 1971
Metal-Dog

27 Jan 1971 – 14 Feb 1972
Metal-Pig

15 Feb 1972 – 2 Feb 1973
Water-Rat

3 Feb 1973 – 22 Jan 1974
Water-Ox

23 Jan 1974 – 10 Feb 1975
Wood-Tiger

11 Feb 1975 – 30 Jan 1976
Wood-Hare

31 Jan 1976 – 17 Feb 1977
Fire-Dragon

18 Feb 1977 – 6 Feb 1978
Fire-Snake

7 Feb 1978 – 27 Jan 1979
Earth-Horse

28 Jan 1979 – 15 Feb 1980
Earth-Sheep

16 Feb 1980 – 4 Feb 1981
Metal-Monkey

5 Feb 1981 – 24 Jan 1982
Metal-Rooster

25 Jan 1982 – 12 Feb 1983
Water-Dog

13 Feb 1983 – 1 Feb 1984
Water-Pig

2 Feb 1984 – 19 Feb 1985
Wood-Rat

20 Feb 1985 – 8 Feb 1986
Wood-Ox

9 Feb 1986 – 28 Jan 1987
Fire-Tiger

29 Jan 1987 – 16 Feb 1988
Fire-Hare

17 Feb 1988 – 5 Feb 1989
Earth-Dragon

6 Feb 1989 – 26 Jan 1990
Earth-Snake

27 Jan 1990 – 14 Feb 1991
Metal-Horse

15 Feb 1991 – 3 Feb 1992
Metal-Sheep

4 Feb 1992 – 22 Jan 1993
Water-Monkey

23 Jan 1993 – 9 Feb 1994
Water-Rooster

10 Feb 1994 – 30 Jan 1995
Wood-Dog

31 Jan 1995 – 18 Feb 1996
Wood-Pig

19 Feb 1996 – 6 Feb 1997
Fire-Rat

7 Feb 1997 – 27 Jan 1998
Fire-Ox

28 Jan 1998 – 15 Feb 1999
Earth-Tiger

16 Feb 1999 – 4 Feb 2000
Earth-Hare

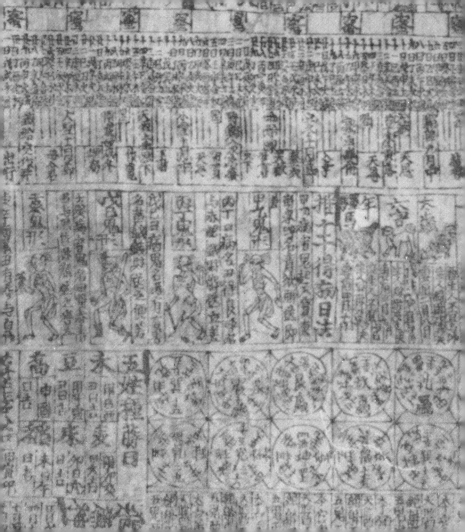